AMERICA LOOKS AHEAD

A Pamphlet Series

No. 1   January 1941   S. SHEPARD JONES, *Editor*

AUSTRALIA AND THE UNITED STATES

By

FRED ALEXANDER

*Head of the Department of History
University of Western Australia*

WORLD PEACE FOUNDATION

BOSTON

1941

WORLD PEACE FOUNDATION

40 Mt. Vernon Street, Boston, Massachusetts

Founded in 1910

THE World Peace Foundation is a non-profit organization which was founded in 1910 by Edwin Ginn, the educational publisher, for the purpose of promoting peace, justice and goodwill among nations. For many years the Foundation has sought to increase public understanding of international problems by an objective presentation of the facts of international relations. This purpose is accomplished principally through its publications and by the maintenance of a Reference Service which furnishes on request information on current international problems. Recently increased attention has been focused on American foreign relations by study groups organized for the consideration of actual problems of policy.

CONTENTS

		Page
FOREWORD by James Grafton Rogers, *Master of Timothy Dwight College, Yale University*	. . . . . .	5
I. INTRODUCTION	. . . .	7
II. CULTURAL RELATIONS	. . . .	11
III. POLITICAL DEVELOPMENTS	. . . . . .	19
IV. STRATEGIC CONSIDERATIONS	. . . . . .	30
V. ECONOMIC FACTORS	. . . .	44
VI. DOUBTS AND DIFFICULTIES	. . . . . .	50
VII. CONDITIONS OF FUTURE COOPERATION	. . . .	58
A SHORT LIST OF BOOKS ON AUSTRALIAN AFFAIRS		66

ACKNOWLEDGMENT

Space does not permit a record of the long list of individual Americans to whom the writer is indebted for frank and stimulating comment on the attitude toward the Pacific of their fellow countrymen—and sometimes of his own; for ready guidance in his search for human and other source materials in many different parts of the United States; and for unfailing encouragement and friendly sympathy. He owes much to a few Australians and New Zealanders whom he encountered, sometimes in strange places, and with whom he was able to exchange ideas and check impressions. Special thanks are due to the Trustees of the World Peace Foundation, who sponsor this booklet; to erstwhile colleagues of the International Secretariat of the Institute of Pacific Relations, and of other institutions with which the writer was temporarily associated in the United States; to the Chancellor and Senate of the University of Western Australia for the Study Leave which permitted his inquiries; and to the Rockefeller Foundation, both for the Fellowship which made those inquiries financially possible and for continued courtesy and consideration in the direction of them. Personal obligations to two men compel recognition. Hubert Whitfeld, most stimulating of Vice-Chancellors, who died firmly convinced that closer relations with the United States was a matter of vital importance to Australia, first directed the writer's thinking toward America. The late Carl L. Alsberg, with whom he was thrown into close contact immediately after his arrival in California, in January 1940, gave generously from a rich fund of wisdom, knowledge and common-sense which more than one Australian learned to respect as among the finest products of American scholarship and American character.

F. A.
New York
December, 1940

FOREWORD

This is the first of a projected series of pamphlets. The Trustees of the World Peace Foundation aim at providing the American public with expert but condensed comment on some of the more important international issues which they are called on to face as the result of the current wars in Europe and in Asia. The Trustees believe that by so doing they serve the purpose for which their Foundation was originally endowed and at the same time meet a present need. Foreign scholars, or others from neighboring countries who are familiar with the American scene, will be among those asked to examine the relationship between the United States and their respective countries. Other writers will be Americans.

It is planned in due course to print comments in pamphlet form on the present and the future position of the United States *vis-à-vis* its near neighbors, Canada and Mexico. Among more distant countries, the Commonwealth of Australia and, incidentally, its sister dominion, New Zealand, are given first appearance in this series, partly because of the lively talk which turns today on Singapore and Japan.

It is worth reminding the reader that this booklet concerns an island continent which is not so very different in area from that of continental United States. Australia is some 3,000 miles from east to west and some 2,000 miles from north to south. Its population of seven millions—approximately that of the City of New York—is concentrated for the most part in the coastal regions of the east, southeast, south, and southwest; much of the interior of the country is "desert" land or is suited for extensive pastoral settlement only. Australians do not pretend that their country will develop into another United States of

America. Some scientists place the upper limit of future Australian population at perhaps thirty millions. New Zealand has a smaller population, not yet two million strong, and exhibits less highly developed manufacturing resources. For all this, it is not difficult to contemplate conditions in which the activities of the English-speaking democracies in this region of the Pacific might be a matter of very great interest to the people of the United States in our attempt to formulate and to apply a Pacific policy, based on our own interests, economic, political, and strategic, in that ocean.

The early place in this series of publications given Australian-American relations is due partly to the presence in the United States of an Australian professor, who had devoted the whole of 1940 to a study of political relations between his country and the United States. Professor Alexander is an Australian of the third generation and a graduate of the University of Melbourne, as well as of Balliol College, Oxford. During the last few years he has been head of the Department of History and, for a period of years, was Dean of the Faculty of Arts in the University of Western Australia. He travelled in Europe as a Rhodes Fellow, was for a short time a member of the Information Section of the Secretariat of the League of Nations, and attended the Thirteenth Assembly of the League as one of the Australian Delegation. He is the author of several works on international and imperial relations, has been a contributor to Australian journals, and a radio commentator at home.

The Trustees have encouraged Professor Alexander to express his opinions freely and frankly. They are not, of course, to be identified with all or any of the views presented. They commend them to the reader as the viewpoint of a well-informed Australian, who is at once a scholar and a spokesman for his country.

JAMES GRAFTON ROGERS

I. INTRODUCTION

When, in February 1940, a distinguished Australian disembarked at Los Angeles from an American trans-Pacific luxury liner and flew to Washington to present his credentials to the President of the United States of America, as the first Australian Minister to Washington, he was given what is usually called a good press. This was not only a personal tribute to the Capital's new "Flying Minister". It also reflected what appeared to be the prevailing American sentiment of friendship and goodwill toward the Australian democracy "down under". In some cases, press comment passed beyond sentiments of goodwill to suggestions of common interest; there was recognition of past associations and even a hint of closer collaboration between the two democracies. Thus the *San Francisco Chronicle* on February 20, 1940:

> This exchange of Ministers between the two countries has an especial interest to California which, from its earliest days, has had closer connection with Australia than any other part of the United States. The Commonwealth is part of our Pacific circle. To us in California it is no remote, dim land. It is before us vividly as a friend and colleague in the advancement of the interests of the Pacific basin. We are heartily glad that the two countries are now to be brought closer together by the establishment of the diplomatic relations that ought, we think, to have been set up long ago.

It would be idle to pretend, however, that, for the vast majority of the American people in February 1940, Australia was much more than a place on the map—a place to be found, not without a little difficulty by some, away at the other end of the Pacific. This distant settlement of a handful of English-speaking people—a mere seven million, the equivalent of the population of New York City—might strike a sympathetic chord in American hearts which vaguely sensed a certain similarity between the American and the Australian way of life. The memories of American veterans of the Great War might occasionally be stirred by thoughts of past associations with Australian "Diggers" on the fields of France. Of the details of Australian life and thought, however, few Americans were well-informed; few, indeed, saw any reason why they should inform themselves about a country with which they were conscious of no material ties and which they could never hope to visit.

And so the Australian Minister arrived, was received with courtesy and friendly interest and, in due course, was allowed to go about the business of his office along with those other privileged dignitaries who are not often seen by Americans but who are believed to live and work, to dine and wine, in the somewhat rarified atmosphere of Washington, D. C. Australia receded into the dim background of the American consciousness, to be resurrected occasionally for brief mention in one or other of the larger newspapers—or even for wider notice if a newsflash from Melbourne or Sydney had the requisite mixture of the melodramatic and the tragi-comic to appeal to "the Desk". As the short American spring of 1940 passed sharply into the hard light of summer, the people of the United States continued to give their rapt attention to the European scene—an attention which seemed to a foreign observer to pass rapidly, like the spring, from the misty stage of detached criticism to a sharp, if exaggerated, realism in which amazement and alarm were not unmixed with panic. Beside the new trans-Atlantic scene and its potential dangers for the United States, even Sino-Japanese news paled into insignificance. The southwest Pacific and Australia were as nothing to Americans in May–June and July.

Yet the summer was not over before an inaugural Clipper, winging its way across the south Pacific, carried with it on its maiden $4\frac{1}{2}$-day flight from California to Auckland as distinguished a band of special correspondents and other American newspapermen as any European country might have been honored to receive. Their 6-day visit to Australia and their return to the

United States via the Netherlands Indies and Singapore gave to the southwest Pacific a line space in American newspapers which could not be explained solely in terms of the American public's interest in the colorful exploits of Pan American Airways.

The autumn brought with it more journalistic flights—some of them pure flights of fancy by columnists and others who sought to read into the dry record of meetings of Secretary of State or President with British Ambassador and Australian Minister news of some far-reaching southwest Pacific agreement. As Indian summer gave way to chill November, the cold winds which stripped the trees in the Mall, and on the wooded environs of the Capital, carried upward many a journalistic or ethereal kite which seemed poised to guide the American Fleet to Singapore.

A bare eight months after the establishment of the Australian Legation in Washington, Australia was, in truth, on the map and in the news—and with it the motley collection of islands, large and small, rich and poor, ranging from Samoa to Singapore, of which Australia has aptly been described as "the central land mass and core," and with which New Zealand, the other British Dominion in the southwest Pacific, is closely associated.

* * * * *

With this as his setting, an Australian student of the American scene in 1940 may, perhaps, thrust on one side a natural feeling of presumption at attempting an analysis of Australian-American relations in a booklet designed primarily for American readers. What seems at first a poor return for a year's hospitality may be justified by the evident growth of interest among the American people in Australia and in neighboring countries. It should, however, be clear to the reader at the outset that the analysis in these pages is made by an Australian who would not wish to hide his nationality while still hoping to preserve his objectivity. An attempt will be made not only to examine the existing relationship between the United States and Australia from the cultural, the political, the strategic and the economic sides, but also to discuss frankly some of the obstacles to closer relations which are suggested to the writer by a knowledge of the state of mind

9

of some of his countrymen and by impressions of American opinion during 1940.

These impressions of American opinion were formed during some eleven months spent in different parts of the United States—on the Pacific Coast, ranging between Los Angeles and Seattle; in New York and Washington; in the Middle West, with a base at Chicago and visits into Iowa and Minnesota; in New England's busy towns and pleasant countryside; and during a flying visit south, to North Carolina, Alabama and Tennessee. Eleven months, spent for the most part in encouraging Americans to air their views about the Pacific in general and about Australia in particular; eleven months, attending half a dozen conferences, formal and informal, and talking elsewhere with professors and politicians, with journalists great and small, with business men and bankers, with labor leaders and ministers of religion, with university students and with a chance collection of taxi-drivers, hotel porters and other members of the American democracy.

What follows is an essay on Australian-American relations and not a compendium of facts about any phase of life in either country or in neighboring regions. There are source books in plenty where such facts may be found, even if these books are not always as accessible as might be wished. Finally, it should be added that, where views are expressed regarding the state of American opinion, no attempt is made to express the view in statistical form. This was not the object of the writer's inquiries throughout the year of his investigation; his method of work would not justify such a presentation of tentative conclusions. Still less is it desired to make any dogmatic predictions regarding the likely state of American opinion tomorrow or the day after. Other would-be prophets may Gallup to victory or defeat on the Australian-American field. For the present writer's purposes, it will be enough in this essay to indicate certain facts and to suggest certain trends of opinion. These, it is submitted, must be taken into account in interpreting the American attitude to Australia, and *vice versa*, in any set of circumstances which is likely to emerge in the reasonably near future.

II. CULTURAL RELATIONS

It has already been suggested that a feeling of good-fellowship exists between the American and the Australian. It is a fact that the two peoples get on together without difficulty. They have some of the characteristics of pioneering peoples even where the pioneering stage has passed. The Australian, like the American, has, as a rule, a directness and a forthright manner—sometimes a certain heartiness—which makes for easy intercourse between them and for a semblance of deep understanding which may or may not exist. The two peoples are readily at home with one another and they share more than a little impatience at the reserve of other peoples—notably at that of the Englishman, in whose initial shyness they are prone to read a conviction of superiority.

All this by way of generalization which cannot cover every case. There are Americans and Americans, just as there are Australians and Australians. It may be that some Melbournians and some New Englanders have more in common with one another and, perhaps, with English country gentry than they have with either West Australian or Iowa farmers—and they are no less good Australians or good Americans for that. The happy fact remains that an ease of relationship exists between the American and the Australian which facilitates closer association, political or economic, between their respective countries, should this closer association commend itself on other grounds. There was a time when American business executives were inclined to talk of Australia as a "labor-ridden land"; today, such criticism would seem to have given way to a certain respect for the speed with which Australians used their political and social machinery to extricate themselves from the more acute phase of the economic depression of the late 'twenties and early 'thirties. Australians, on their side, have not hesitated to criticize what they are pleased to call the material basis of American civilization; they have nevertheless shown themselves ready enough to emulate and even to envy the material achievements of that same American civilization. There are, in short, no serious prejudices to be broken down between the two nations; there are no deep-rooted suspicions to cloud the issue when negotiations between governments begin, or to preclude negotiations altogether.

All this makes a good beginning. Sympathy and goodwill go a long way toward understanding; they may, however, stop far short of that goal. This certainly has been true of the past relations between the American and the Australian democracies. There are few Australians who can today claim more than a superficial appreciation of American life and thought. There are perhaps fewer Americans who have made the effort to understand Australia.

Australians are the less easily excused for their shortcomings in this respect. As a people, they have had a powerful incentive to seek to understand the people of the United States, if only because the march of events during the twentieth century has brought more and more Australians into daily contact with the fruits of American thought and of American labor. For a generation or so America has meant more to Australians than Australia has to Americans. In their ordinary lives, Australians have long been familiar with the more superficial features of American life. Many Australian enterprises have sought to copy American methods and to reach American standards of efficiency in mass production. There are few Australian boys who cannot readily distinguish between the makes—and, in a good many cases, between the internal idiosyncracies—of American automobiles. Some surprisingly high results might also be yielded by an Australian-wide quiz on the physical attributes and the private lives of American movie stars.

But motor car and oil salesmen and Hollywood producers, admirable though each may be in his way, are not the most reliable missionaries of American civilization. American cities

12

contain more than garages and gangsters; American universities do not all revolve around the activities of burly football coaches and glamorous "co-eds". It is at least intelligible that many of the Australian rank-and-file, who are faithful patrons of the "movies", should believe to the contrary. For the few, enlightenment has come by way of reading or of trans-Pacific travel. Most of the leading business executives in Australia have visited the United States. Many Australian scholars have also benefited by the books and by the generous travelling facilities supplied by American trust funds. There is even a school of Australian educationists who sometimes seem to regard American educational methods as something to be transplanted in their entirety to the Australian scene. But these are exceptions which prove the rule. The great majority of educated Australians have continued to receive their intellectual inspiration from British, European and Australian sources, not from the United States. Most of the professors in one or other of the six Australian universities have had post-graduate training in Great Britain or in Europe; only a few can boast an American degree or its equivalent. Naturally enough, a professor tends to advise most of his own outstanding graduates to go abroad to Great Britain or to Europe, to countries where he may provide them with personal introductions. And so the wheel comes round full circle.

What is true of professional education applies equally well to other forms of cultural life in Australia. Australian art and literature owe much to English and European influence and to their own sturdy independence; they owe little to American sources. Australian specialists may claim an acquaintance with American publications in their own fields, yet even they display a preference for British or Australian texts, though some American educational publishers find enough in the Australian market to support peripatetic representatives in the country. American books for the general reader do not seriously compete with those from British houses. And this though there is no Australian customs duty on books and—in peacetime—no other prohibition or limitation on the import of books or periodicals from overseas which

13

do not offend against official canons of decency. An American best-seller may occasionally capture the Australian market, on which American thrillers and the poorer type of periodical normally find a ready sale, but the Australian reads for preference books with an Australian or the English background with which he is more or less familiar. Once more the vicious circle.

The truth is that Australians have looked to Great Britain and to Europe for cultural inspiration when they have not been content to rely on their own native genius. In this they have behaved very much as Americans did for generations until the beginning of the present century. The older civilization has always had a magnetic influence upon the new, especially when its attraction has been reinforced by influences of race and language. Upon Australians, the racial influence has been considerable. Though the label "98% British" is a gross exaggeration —a figure in the eighties would be nearer the mark—the Australian society is mainly Anglo-Saxon, and is exclusively European in race. Early conflicts between European and Oriental in the gold rush days of the eighteen fifties and later in the 'nineties convinced the young Australian democracy that its social and economic ideals would be threatened by the competition of cheap labor provided by a race which could not easily be assimilated. The White Australia Policy thus found its way to general acceptance; by the use of a prescribed "dictation test", Asiatics were excluded in fact, though not in name, and Australians deliberately reduced to a minimum contacts with the Pacific which might indirectly have qualified the exclusively European influences upon their culture.

The United States pursued a somewhat different course in its relations with Far Eastern countries, with the result that the Far East has come to mean more to Americans, emotionally and culturally than it has ever meant to Australians. The effect of American trade expansion was not a negligible factor, but the influence which brought the Pacific into the minds of the majority of the people of the United States was that of American missionaries in China and in Japan. The reports of these missionaries to

14

the members of their American churches, the visits to the United States of Chinese and, to a lesser extent, of Japanese students, established a line of cultural communication between Americans and these two peoples of the western Pacific which has had a profound effect on American sentiment and, sometimes, on United States policy in the Pacific.

The direction of this American line of cultural communication across the Pacific is, however, important. It ran due west or northwest from the Californian coast; rarely did it go southwest. The nationwide interest of the American people in the western Pacific was, until the middle of 1940, almost exclusively an interest in China and Japan—with some attention given to Russia by those American missionaries of a different religion who operated chiefly in the home field. Before the outbreak of the war in September 1939, it was rare, indeed, for the range of American interest to take in the southwest Pacific. One of the most surprising results of the writer's investigations on the Pacific coast from January to April, 1940, was the relatively slight response he obtained to questions regarding American interest in the Netherlands Indies or Malaya. As an Australian, he was forewarned not to expect detailed knowledge of his own distant country but, given the existing dependence of the United States upon the East Indies and Malaya for supplies of important strategic raw materials—tin, rubber, cinchona bark—the prevailing ignorance and apathy regarding this region of the southwest Pacific demanded explanation.

The explanation is not far to seek. It may be found partly in the fact that the considerable trade from the East Indies to the United States is carried in foreign bottoms and that it is concentrated in the hands of a few large concerns. The American housewife wielding her can-opener in the kitchen, her husband changing his tires in the garage, were neither of them moved to think of the flow of the raw materials which contributed so appreciably to these aspects of the twentieth century way of American life. But the explanation goes deeper. There were no American missionaries in the Netherlands Indies and in neighboring regions. There the work of Christianizing the Malays was left largely to Netherlands, to German and to British missions, though American Lutherans were given a financial interest during the international complication of 1914–18. Farther south, the souls of the Australian Aboriginals were left to the care of Australian missions. American anthropologists were the nearest approach to American missionaries who sought to visit this rapidly dwindling race, now a mere 78,000 in a total Australian population of over 7,000,000; and the anthropologist is concerned to recapture the ways of the past rather than to prepare for the life hereafter.

It is worth insisting, moreover, that even where American cultural and sentimental associations with Pacific countries were close and their influence upon national policy correspondingly strong, those associations and that influence were less powerful than the attraction which came from the racial, the cultural and the traditional ties between the United States and Europe. It has not been easy for Australian observers to grasp this fact. Australians have been misled by the prominence given by the American people, through both their official and their unofficial representatives, to the depth of American feeling on certain trans-Pacific questions. Demonstrations in recent years of friendship for China, of suspicion of Japan and of hostility to aggression in Manchuria or in China proper have created the impression abroad that the American people were united in supporting a well considered long-term policy in the western Pacific. One reason why Australian observers were so misled is that they failed to grasp the fundamental fact that, to the American people, as to themselves, the issues outside their own country which seemed really to strike at the roots of their being arose from European and not from Asiatic sources.

In such efforts as they made to establish close contact and informed understanding between them, the Australian and the American peoples received little assistance from the newspapers of their respective countries. The reluctance of American papers (with some important but rare exceptions) to maintain special correspondents in Australia is intelligible if regrettable; the

16

willingness of Australian newspaper proprietors to be content, until quite recently, with an inadequate service of American news lays them open to a censure which may be the more sharp because of the relatively high standards of Australian journalism and because of the quality and the range of the Australian news service from Great Britain and Europe. The high cost of cables between the United States and Australia retarded improvement. A rearrangement of cable services took place in 1935; even then, however, Australian press representatives in the United States were limited to some 3,000 words a week. It is only since the outbreak of the war with Nazi Germany that cable news from the United States to Australia has been reorganized in such a way that all the leading Australian newspapers are supplied with a basic service which is supplemented by cabled messages from special American correspondents of individual papers or groups of papers in the several Australian States.

The apparent paradox which emerges from this survey of cultural associations between the United States and Australia is, therefore, that it has been through Europe that these two nations at opposite ends of the Pacific Ocean have in the past made their most important contacts. It was by their common attraction to the European source of much of their civilization—and even by their resistance to that attraction—that Americans and Australians were from time to time made conscious of the importance which each might have for the other. There is deep significance in the fact that Australians are still best known to Americans by the meetings of "Doughboys" and "Diggers" on the battlefields of France; it is more than a historical accident that it was another European war which, in the second half of 1940, gave to American policy in the southwest Pacific, and thereby to Australian-American relations, a vividness and a reality which they had never possessed before.

* * * * *

To the generalization of the last paragraph an important qualification should at once be set. While it is submitted that the basic concern of the American people with European rather

17

than Pacific issues persisted down to the outbreak of the war against Nazi Germany, and was strengthened by that conflict in ways to be noted in the next section, there had been forces at work within Australia for more than a decade which had already shown signs of a new orientation of Australian thought and opinion regarding other Pacific countries before war broke out in September 1939. A small but influential school of Australian opinion has for years clamored for greater attention to the thought and the culture of other peoples in Australia's own geographic region. Some of the desire for closer relations with other Pacific countries was motivated by economic or by strategic considerations, but it also had what for want of a better word may be called its cultural side. The desire of a small group of educators to take advantage of American experiments in conditions resembling those of some parts of Australia provoked a generous response from American Foundations and has had some levelling influence on Australian education. Meanwhile, the influence upon Australia of American material achievement continued; the social experiments which grew out of the depression in the United States also stimulated especial interest among an Australian people who liked to think of themselves as pioneers in social legislation and who had, in fact, been engaged for several decades in rapid acceleration of their own industrial development.

This gradual reorientation of Australian thought toward the Pacific in the 'twenties and 'thirties has been an important predisposing factor, making possible far-reaching political developments under pressure of wartime events. It may, nevertheless, be asserted that the outbreak of the war with Nazi Germany found both the Australian and the American peoples without any deep knowledge of one another—without that informed understanding which might quietly reinforce the bonds of sentiment and might help to translate gestures of good-fellowship into joint action to mutual advantage.

The fact may be regretted by advocates of Australian-American cooperation; it should, however, be faced fairly and squarely by friends on both sides of the Pacific.

III. POLITICAL DEVELOPMENTS

Since the political institutions and the political practice of any people are one expression of its culture, the argument of the preceding pages suggests the theme of this section. The political practice of the Australian democracy has been based chiefly on that of Great Britain, despite the fact that its constitutional organization since 1900 has been greatly influenced by that of the United States, which served as a model for many features of the Australian Federal Constitution established at the turn of the century. In domestic affairs Australians have sought and, in large measure, have succeeded in making their own standards. These social and economic standards have tended to dominate the thinking of Australians to the exclusion of matters of foreign policy, in regard to which, until quite recently, the majority of the Australian people were generally indifferent. They were content enough to leave even major matters to the British Government, except where a direct and immediate Australian interest was seen to be involved. They were reluctant to allow themselves to be distracted from the considerable tasks of economic and social development at home by involvement in schemes for closer political association abroad. As a people, they gave little attention to theoretical discussions of international organization and were unwilling to accept far-reaching commitments to joint action, even in the Pacific region, in regard to which their political approach suggests some striking similarities with, and some sharp differences from, that of the American people.

The two points in this analysis which may seem to call for elaboration are, on the one hand, the insistence of the Australian on his freedom from interference in grappling with his local problems and, on the other, his ready and cheerful acceptance of a

19

measure of external direction in foreign affairs. The inconsistency is more apparent than real, for the second characteristic really stems from the first. Australia's very considerable economic progress of the last half-century, during which the country has been transformed from almost exclusive reliance upon primary production of wool, wheat, dairy produce, fruits, gold and other metals, into an industrialized nation in which more than 20% of the population is directly dependent on secondary industry— this has been made possible by the financial assistance of London, by the continued accessibility of British markets to Australian raw materials, and by the territorial security which was ensured by the British connection, as visually represented to Australians by the might of the British Navy. Australian nationalism has been different in character from the dominion nationalism of Canada and of South Africa. With occasional exceptions, it has concerned itself less with assertions of theoretical equality or with the dangers of external involvement through British foreign policy. Function rather than status has interested the minority of Australians who have bothered themselves over the niceties of inter-Imperial relations. Anxious to get on with the job at home, most Australians have shown little interest in the refining of terms to describe a relationship with Great Britain and with the other members of the British Commonwealth, which they felt to work well enough in practice. Did it not provide them with all the freedom they wished to manage their own affairs, while preserving sufficient unity in matters of common concern to ensure the diplomatic and, if need be, the armed support of the British Commonwealth to aid in maintaining Australia's security? In the economic reorganization of the last half-century, moreover, experience had taught Australians that even a measure of British financial control was not sufficient to prevent the growth of tariff walls protecting Australian industries by duties which were only less high against British than against foreign manufacturers. Both organized labor and employing groups were content enough with a state of affairs which assured to the one reasonable standards of living and to the other reasonable profits, in a condition of comparative security from external attack. All political parties gave more than lip-service to the ideals of Australian nationhood but none ventured to proclaim distinctively Australian foreign or defense policies which gravely threatened the unity of the British Commonwealth or which seriously challenged the *de facto* direction of Australian foreign policy from Downing Street.

From this condition of preoccupation with the problems of local development, Australians were rudely shocked by the events of 1914. They responded readily and effectively. The record of some 329,000 volunteers for overseas service, in a population which was then only five millions, showed what the combined influence of idealism, sentiment and self-interest could produce from even a provincially-minded people when the hour of crisis came. But when the excitement was over and Armistice had given place to Peace Conference and post-war problems, Australians, like Americans, reverted readily enough to type in their attitude to the outside world. It was difficult in the 'twenties to persuade Australian audiences that they had either a material or a moral interest in taking an active part in international politics. Officially, Australia accepted membership in the League of Nations; theoretically, Australian statesmen claimed a right of independent judgment on all major matters of international politics. In practice, the Australian public displayed even less interest than the American public in the European policies of Great Britain during the first fifteen years after the Great War. Australian Governments spasmodically asserted their right to be informed of British policy and of British action; there was, however, no outward sign that any Australian Government was in the habit of forming independent judgments and of pressing its opinions on Downing Street.

The preoccupation of the Australian with his local problems in the 'twenties was more the result of unconscious provincialism than of active isolationism. To this extent his attitude may be distinguished from the prevailing American sentiment in the same period. It was less a matter of deliberate policy than of accidental

21

circumstance—it was the by-product of a period of active industrial development, under cover of a high tariff, in an era of peace and security. The distinction between provincial detachment and isolationist aloofness is illustrated well enough in the policy of the powerful Australian Labor Party which appeared to be increasingly isolationist in its attitude to foreign affairs but which was, in fact, primarily concerned to avoid interference with its local program of social reform and industrialization.

There was little to bring Australia and the United States into political contact during the post-war years, when demands of local development determined the international outlook of the one country and pressure of isolationist sentiment that of the other. When the two *were* forced into political contact over Pacific questions, interest and sentiment appeared to divide rather than to unite Australian and United States representatives. In the negotiations preliminary to the Washington Conference of 1921–22, the United States Government did not at first contemplate Australian or other dominion representation at the conference. Australian statesmen, moreover, unlike their Canadian cousins, did what they could in British Commonwealth discussions of 1921 to secure the renewal of the Anglo-Japanese Alliance. This with no intention of directing that alliance against the United States or against American interests. Australians were mindful, however, that from Japan might come the one threat to their security which remained after Germany had been ousted from the Pacific. Past experience had shown that an Anglo-Japanese alliance could protect instead of endangering south Pacific trade routes; Australians sought to perpetuate that state of affairs as long as they could.

When overruled by the weight of opinion in Great Britain and Canada, Australians accepted the Washington Treaties of 1922 as a satisfactory alternative. If a multilateral agreement instead of a bilateral alliance would give peace and stability to the Pacific, it was readily acceptable to Australia. Trade was increasing between Australia and both the United States and Japan; disarmament was in the mouths of most politicians; there seemed to be every reason to go ahead with local development and no cause for seeking closer political associations with any other Pacific country.

No special reasons, therefore, suggested themselves for strengthening political relations beween the United States and Australia as long as the 'twenties and early 'thirties seemed to be carrying the world in the direction of lasting peace and general disarmament. When the trend was checked and clouds began to appear on the international horizon, first in Manchuria and then in North China, some positive obstacles to such closer relations between the United States and Australia presented themselves in the diverging attitudes of the two countries toward Japan. The reaction of many Australians to the Japanese invasion of Manchuria was similar to that which most Americans were to adopt years after, when Hitler invaded Austria. It was too bad, but what could Australia do about it? Australians even found a little selfish consolation in the thought that, when the Japanese were minded to commit an act of aggression, they should have selected the mainland of northern China rather than the islands of the southwest Pacific. When Australians did give much attention to the complicated negotiations on the Manchurian question, moreover, they had difficulty in following United States policy. The idealism of Mr. Stimson and his desire to stop Japan were appreciated; there were Australian as there were British critics of Foreign Secretary Sir John Simon for his cold reception of the Secretary of State's suggested collaboration on the Manchurian question. But Australians viewed the prospect of Anglo-American collaboration in the Far East chiefly in terms of their own security. If Japan were provoked and were stung into naval retaliation, all British communities in the Pacific would be in the danger zone. British naval strength in that Ocean being no longer what it once had been, Australian observers were disposed to ask themselves the direct question whether Anglo-American diplomatic collaboration on the Manchurian issue would automatically bring with it an assurance of American naval assistance in the event of Japanese retaliation against British possessions. When this question failed to produce a clear affirmative answer, those Australians who had diverted their attention momentarily from the domestic scene to the northwest Pacific were disposed to prefer what they felt might be the reality of a revived Anglo-Japanese collaboration, effectively restraining Japanese aggression, to the shadow of Anglo-American diplomatic collaboration which might be based on words, and words alone.

It is now generally accepted that no single incident was more influential in damaging Anglo-American relations in the decade preceding the outbreak of the war with Nazi Germany than the Simon-Stimson affair. Rightly or wrongly, Americans felt that they had been let down by the British; the incident was freely discussed and the somewhat *ex parte* statement in Mr. Stimson's book *The Far Eastern Crisis* was widely circulated. Happily, Australian-American relations were not directly affected by the incident; the extent to which official and unofficial Australian opinion had supported British action was not clear and Americans directed the full force of their criticism against Sir John Simon and his colleagues, with whom, indeed, the decision had rested. The Manchurian incident is, nevertheless, worth recording in an analysis of the political relations between the United States and Australia, because it emphasized the absence of what the present writer regards as an essential predisposing condition of Australian-American political collaboration on Pacific questions. This condition is the readiness of both parties to base their collaboration not merely on sentiment and goodwill but on a conviction of common interest which will carry both peoples, if necessary, from gestures into action. This positive condition was not present in 1931–32. It remained absent even as long as six months after the outbreak of war with Nazi Germany in September 1939.

In the years following 1932 the Government and the people of Australia, like the Government and the people of Great Britain, learned to appreciate the difficulties involved, and the slight chance of success, in attempting to restrain Japan from within. They nevertheless retained their reluctance to provoke Japan into "mad-dog" action in the southwest Pacific by any form of economic or diplomatic pressure undertaken in conjunction with another nation which, if the time came to resist Japanese retaliation, might lack either the naval strength or the willingness to collaborate fully in opposing that retaliation. Accordingly, when the Australian Government decided, in 1939, to establish an Australian Legation in Washington, it announced that this Legation would be followed by another at Tokyo. Mr. R. G. Casey had not been six months in the United States when the Prime Minister of Australia selected Sir John Latham, Chief Justice of the High Court, to serve as Minister to Japan. These appointments implemented the policy outlined by Prime Minister Robert Menzies in his first broadcast after he took office in April 1939. He said then that, while on European affairs, Australia must be largely guided by the United Kingdom Government's knowledge and affected by its decisions, in the Pacific, Australia (and New Zealand) had primary responsibilities and took the primary risks. To Australia, what the Englishman called the Far East was "the Near North". In the Pacific, Australia must regard herself as a principal, providing her own information and maintaining her own diplomatic contacts. All her consultations with the rest of the Empire regarding Pacific matters must be on the basis that Australia (and New Zealand) bore the primary risks in the Pacific. It may be assumed that this policy was seen in action when the British Government decided, in August 1940, to close the Burma Road for three months to avoid Japanese action against Hong Kong and elsewhere. It was reported that the British Government had acted with the concurrence of, if not also under pressure from, the Government of Australia.

Meanwhile, American policy in the western Pacific had moved but slowly from an attitude of moral indignation at Japanese aggression combined with unwillingness to assume positive obligations to check that aggression. The research work of American scholars has now revealed the fact that even when Mr. Stimson was most actively seeking Sir John Simon's collaboration over Manchuria, President Hoover had emphatically stated his refusal to concur in any form of pressure upon Japan other than that of moral suasion. During the five years that followed, in their reaction to the abortive Anglo-American negotiations of 1931-32, the people of the United States swung still further away from Far Eastern commitments. Evacuation of American nationals and abandonment of American interests was the prevailing sentiment. There was nothing in this to make for closer political collaboration with an Australian democracy which was beginning to watch the Far Eastern situation with an increasing awareness of what its own isolated position would be if the Japanese should transfer their attentions from the Chinese mainland to the south Pacific. The policy which seemed to be indicated to Australians was not to seek active association with an American nation which appeared to be withdrawing from the western Pacific, but to strengthen home defense and to hope that Great Britain would avoid European hostilities which would limit British naval strength in the Pacific.

It was in this state of mind that the Australian people drifted into the tragic days of Munich, 1938. The Czechoslovakian "settlement" of September was to prove the turning point in Australian-American relations, as in so many other matters. In its immediate effects, however, Munich did little to strengthen the ties, either sentimental or material, between the United States and Australia. For the great majority of the Australian people accepted the Chamberlain policy of appeasement. They were reluctant to be forced out of their preoccupation with local affairs to fight in another European conflict; some, though not all, Australians were also sharply aware of the difference between the conditions of 1914-18 and the effects which a new war might have upon Australian security if Japan joined the Axis Powers. A small minority of Australians—among whom the writer was one—took the platform against the Munich settlement, arguing, among other things, that its moral effect on neutral, including American, opinion would offset the strategic gains of a respite from war. But those voicing such views were a small minority and most Australians regarded the bitter American denunciation

26

of Munich as the unrealistic criticism of a people who were themselves unwilling to accept commitments but who were in the happy position of being free from danger of attack.

The aftermath of Munich in the western Pacific seemed to widen the gulf between Australian interests and United States policy. American suspicions of British policy in the Far East, which had been smouldering since 1931–32, were fanned into flame by the "betrayal" of Czechoslovakia. There was an increasing reluctance to "pull British and French chestnuts out of the fire" in the Far East. When war broke out in Europe in September 1939, these suspicions did not abate. They were strengthened by the dominance which European developments then came to have on the minds of the American people. As long as the American people were determined not to be associated with the European conflict in any way, a vigorous policy in the western Pacific was doubly dangerous. It not only invited war in defense of Far Eastern interests which many Americans were reluctant to accept; the Far East might also prove a back door to European involvement.

The writer landed in San Francisco in January 1940, on the eve of the expiration of the 1911 trade treaty between the United States and Japan. In the ten weeks that followed, as he moved up and down the Pacific coast, he found an almost universal hostility to Japanese policy and strong demonstrations of friendship for China. This emotional "set-up" was unmistakable. On the other hand, it was rare indeed to find a Pacific coast American who was prepared to carry aid to China to a point where war with Japan might result. The commercial and shipping minority on the coast were especially emphatic on this matter. In their less guarded moments, they spoke frankly of Japan as a good customer of the United States, and they did not hesitate to present Japan as a desirable alternative to the Soviet Union in the role of dominant power of the western Pacific. Even apart from this minority, there was no evidence to suggest to an Australian observer that more than a small minority of Americans in that part of the country which was nearest the Pacific and where Japanese

27

migration had created much ill-feeling, was prepared to translate anti-Japanese or pro-Chinese gestures into financial or economic measures which would entail the risk of war. There was no conviction of vital American interests across the Pacific; there was, moreover, a growing concern at the outcome of events in Europe.

In Australia, on the other hand, the course of the war with Nazi Germany stimulated a good deal of thinking on long-term as well as short-term policy in the Pacific. The immediate effects of the war upon Australia had been cushioned in advance by the Russo-German Pact of August 23, 1939, and the temporary diplomatic isolation of Japan which this effected. Australians nevertheless entered the war—only a few hours after the United Kingdom declaration—with their eyes open. They realized what the limitations of British naval strength might mean at any time for the British Dominions, Australia and New Zealand, virtually isolated in the southwest Pacific. Their response to the danger was fourfold: to accelerate their preparations for home defense, by land, by air and by sea; to give what they could in men and materials to assist the British war effort in Europe, in the Mediterranean and in Singapore; to avoid any provocative action *vis-a-vis* Japan which was likely to invite an extension of the war to the Pacific. At the same time, they were ready and anxious to explore fully the possibilities of closer relations with other Pacific countries, out of which might come not only a lessening of the immediate danger in the southwest Pacific but also the prospect of permanent peace in the whole Pacific area.

The Australian Government's determination to adhere to its pre-war decision, by establishing the Legation at Washington early in 1940, did in fact reflect a growing conviction among the Australian people that, whatever the outcome of the war in Europe, the future would increase Australia's associations, political and cultural, as well as economic and strategic, with the other countries of the Pacific area. After the first shock of the post-Munich period was over and the drift to war was accepted as a highly dangerous but perhaps inevitable development, the Australian people accepted the fact that they were not to be left alone to grapple with their domestic problems regardless of the rest of the world. In the stocktaking that followed, assets and liabilities in the Pacific were examined more carefully than ever before. In this appraisal of assets, there was more than a little wishful thinking in some quarters—wishful thinking prompted by ignorance of the realities of American politics and by failure to appreciate the gap which may separate emotional gesture from positive commitment in American foreign policy. There were some Australians who convinced themselves without difficulty that, in the last resort, if the worst came to the worst, "Uncle Sam would not let down his cousins across the Pacific." The majority, while watching with fresh interest the trend of opinion in the United States, from month to month, were concerned primarily with the task of strengthening their own defenses. On Australia's part, there was dimly developing a certain appreciation of the basic condition mentioned above, that if collaboration were to come between the democracies of the Pacific region, it would come not as the result of fine words, based on generous sentiments, but in recognition of common interests and in respect for the value of individual contributions to a common cause. As the war against Nazi Germany passed from its initial stalemate to the dark days of May-June 1940, strategic necessity rather than wishful dreaming dominated the minds of the Australian Government and of the great majority of the Australian people.

By May-June, the machinery for closer political relations between the United States had been set up, with an Australian Minister established in Washington and an American Minister on his way to Canberra. No great progress in closer collaboration between the two democracies could, however, be effected until the American as well as the Australian people had been shocked by the course of the war in Europe into a revision of their thinking on strategic issues, in the Pacific no less than in the Atlantic.

IV. STRATEGIC CONSIDERATIONS

Until the course of the war against Nazi Germany forced Americans as well as Australians to re-examine carefully the aims and objects of their defense policies, there was no justification for saying that the two peoples had any real appreciation of the extent to which the strategic interests of their countries might coincide. Before the war, Australian defense was closely correlated with that of the British Empire; Australian advocates of a more specifically regional defense program were viewed with some suspicion by their fellow countrymen. In the United States, it is true that the Pacific was recognized as a field of special activity as long as French and British navies held the Atlantic, but a sharp distinction was drawn between activity within the triangle of the Aleutian Islands, Hawaii and the Panama Canal—to be defended at all costs—and operations west of Hawaii. The latter were presented as extremely difficult because of inadequate western Pacific bases; they were discussed, if at all, as part of a long, costly and difficult war against Japan which would be conducted in the last resort in Japanese waters, where a sensible advantage would be enjoyed by the Japanese unless superior naval strength could be brought against them. In these discussions, the Philippines were felt to be a liability rather than an asset; the implied inference was that a choice in fact lay between a purely defensive strategy based on protection of the triangle and a deliberate and difficult offensive—an attempt to anticipate the inevitable, to "go out and sink the Japanese fleet." Though other courses of action were doubtless fully explored in official circles, semi-official and popular discussions of naval strategy as late as 1939 and the early part of 1940 gave no prominence to the possibility of a "holding war" in the southwest Pacific designed to prevent

Japanese control of the oil, tin, rubber and iron of the Netherlands Indies and Malaya. The greater part of a year of war in Europe was required before public opinion in Australia and in the United States was brought to appreciate something of the significance which the southwest Pacific might in this way have for both countries. In naval strategy, as in political attitudes, it was developments in Europe which were primarily responsible for bringing the United States and Australia closer to one another during the course of 1940.

American opinion on the subject of naval strategy in the Pacific may be said to have passed through three phases between the outbreak of war in September 1939, and the end of 1940. In the first phase, down to the fall of France, pre-war opinion as described in the previous paragraph persisted with little change. There were, indeed, differences in emphasis. Some Americans wished to anticipate the day of Philippine independence in 1946, by an immediate intimation of unwillingness to participate in any form of naval action in the western Pacific. Others preferred a show of strength in the western Pacific as a means of bluffing Japan and of aiding China, without in fact laying the United States open to any risk of war. A third group, which was prepared for an active offensive against Japan, commanded little if any support. Successive attempts by the United States Navy to secure Congressional approval for funds to fortify Guam failed largely because it was felt that such a step would be, in effect, a threat to Japan in her home waters. As public attention centered on the course of the war in Europe, there was no evidence to show that a vigorous naval policy in the Pacific would command public support. The strategic significance of the southwest Pacific received little attention in the first six months of the war, though Japanese feelers in April produced the Hull declaration on April 17 regarding the *status quo* of the Netherlands Indies. The stepping-up of American rearmament programs also brought strategic raw materials under discussion and, with that discussion, came signs of the beginning of a belated public interest in the East Indian territories and Malaya from which the United States drew 75% of its tin, 85% of its rubber and nearly all of its cinchona bark for quinine.

The effect upon American strategy in the Pacific of the *Blitzkrieg* in western Europe and of the fall of France was much more serious than was realized at the time. The first reaction of Americans to the realization that they might not be able to depend much longer on the British Navy to police the Atlantic was to consider withdrawal of the United States Fleet from the Pacific to the Caribbean. Hemisphere defense rapidly became "a blessed word" with which to calm fears of trans-Atlantic invasion. The writer recalls conversations he had with newspapermen, politicians and officials in Washington at the end of May—conversations in which the constantly recurring question was the fate of the British fleet. During this period there were persistent rumors that the United States Navy would shortly move eastward from Hawaii. A New York newspaper with a large circulation openly abandoned its strongly anti-Japanese policy to plead for an accomodation with Japan which would avoid a war on two fronts. Similar views were expressed by columnists and others who were sometimes less pessimistic about the course of British resistance in the Atlantic and across the Channel but who regarded any American action in the Pacific as a limitation upon the assistance which could and should be sent to the British across the Atlantic.

These fears were reinforced by the fall of France. Uncertainty as to the fate of the French Navy heightened the importance popularly allotted to Atlantic defenses. It was not until after events at Oran and at Alexandria had determined that the greater part of the French fleet would not be at Hitler's command that it became clear that the Administration in Washington had successfully resisted pressure to transfer the greater part of the United States Navy eastward from Hawaii. As the worst fears of June gave way to a less emotional and a more rational appraisal of the new situation across the Atlantic, the pendulum began to swing back a little toward the Pacific. The swing of opinion continued under the influence of effective British resistance to threatened

Nazi invasion. With the stimulus of the destroyers-for-bases agreement of August, American opinion moved to a point considerably beyond what had seemed the outside limits of American public interest before the *Blitzkrieg* of May. It was not long, in fact, before the eyes of Americans were directed to Singapore and to other British (and Australian) bases in the southwest Pacific.

A sharp contrast may, therefore, be drawn between the short-term and the long-term influence of Nazi victories in France upon the American public's conception of United States naval strategy in the Pacific. The immediate effect of the European events of May-June was to distract American attention from the Pacific. It seemed that previous reluctance to invite hostilities with Japan had been transformed into a determination under no circumstances to act in the western Pacific while the future was uncertain across the Atlantic. The ultimate effect was very different. The threat to the British Navy in the Atlantic brought to many Americans the first clear realization that Great Britain was their first line of defense. From this developed a new conception of the significance of outer lines of defense and of the importance of sea power. The new conception was effectively illustrated for the American people by the acquisition of bases in British islands from Newfoundland to the Caribbean and Guiana. The islands were near enough for the significance of the bases to be apparent to Americans; the underlying principle was none the less clearly implied. It was not surprising that a few weeks after the destroyers-for-bases deal had received public support that speculation began as to its possible extension into the Pacific, not merely to guard the Canal but also to set up outer lines of defense west of Hawaii.

Related developments in Europe and Asia served to sharpen this rising American interest in outer lines of defense. One consequence of the fall of France had been Japanese activity in Indo-China. The threat to the Netherlands Indies was thereby transformed from the field of speculation to the realm of reality. With Holland under Nazi military control, moreover, a German-Japanese agreement regarding Netherlands overseas possessions

33

was readily assumed. Meanwhile, the rapid acceleration of the tempo of American rearmament after the fall of France re-emphasized the significance of the strategic raw materials obtained by the United States from the southwest Pacific.

It was against this background of quickening American interest in the southwest Pacific that the German and Japanese leaders threw their provocative announcement of September 27 that what had once been an Anti-Comintern Pact had now been transformed into a military alliance between Germany, Italy and Japan, threatening united action against the United States should it interfere with or block their expansion program. The apparent objective of the new treaty was to intimidate the United States and, from Japan's viewpoint, to check the rising tide of American public sentiment for action against that country. If such was the purpose of the agreement it was based on an entirely false reading of the psychology of the American people. The actual effect was to stiffen public resistance in the United States; it also provided a convenient way of return for some of those writers who, in the dark days of June, had declared themselves in favor of a deal with Japan as a necessary means of avoiding a war on two fronts.

The effect of this upon discussion of American strategy in the Pacific from late September to the end of 1940 was twofold. In the first place, there was evidence of an increase in the number of those—probably a minority within official circles, as undoubtedly they still were elsewhere—who favored an early all-out offensive against Japan to destroy the Japanese Navy while Great Britain continued to resist across the Atlantic and before Japan could throw into a war with the United States the 40,000 ton battleships which she was reported to be building in unspecified numbers. More significant for the student of Australian-American relations was the second result of the Japanese-Axis agreement of late September. A new importance was popularly ascribed to rumored naval base arrangements between the United States, Great Britain and Australia. A crop of magazine articles and press and radio comment appeared, discussing the possibility

that British-American understanding in the southwest Pacific
would enable the United States Navy to check further southward
expansion by Japan with much less strain than would be involved
in the launching of an all-out offensive in Japanese waters and,
possibly, without war at all. It was difficult for a layman to
determine the extent to which such speculation reflected official
discussions, but there were indications which suggested that
naval authorities were more fully exploring the possibilities of
operations based on the southwest Pacific—partly because of
conviction that such operations might, in the long run, be as
valuable as and less dangerous than offensive tactics farther north
and partly, perhaps, because of a growing conviction that, on
grounds of high policy, the Administration might at any moment
decide on collaboration with Great Britain and the British
Dominions in the southwest Pacific and might call on the United
States Navy to foot the bill—in other words, to be prepared to
implement a political decision by the necessary strategic arrangements.

The strategic conception which appeared to result from these
discussions regarding British-American collaboration in the
southwest Pacific was based on one or other of two assumptions.
The first assumption was that, on the outbreak of hostilities, a
portion of the United States Navy would already be located in
the southwest Pacific and so in a position to interpose itself
against any naval force which the Japanese could send at relatively
short notice from Hainan or from Indo-Chinese ports to protect
a Japanese army invading the Netherlands Indies. Alternatively,
if the United States Navy were not located in the southwest
Pacific at the beginning of a Japanese drive to the Indies, the existing naval and air defenses of the Netherlanders were assumed to
be sufficient to prevent Japanese occupation of the more vital parts
of their islands. Singapore was also deemed capable of lengthy
resistance to both or either forms of attack to which it might be
subjected—by sea and air bombardment and by land operations
directed from Indo-China via Thailand (Siam) over the difficult
terrain of the intervening isthmus. Meantime, the Japanese

would be harassed by the raiding tactics of such British and American submarine, seaplane and surface vessels as might be based on Hong Kong and Manila at the outbreak of war. The implication was that, while the Japanese were meeting with this resistance, United States naval forces would be speeding toward Singapore and the Indies—and to Manila, unless it had been decided temporarily to relinquish control of the Philippines. They would come either directly westward from Hawaii or by a southern route via Pago Pago in Samoa, British islands in the south Pacific, and the eastern and northern waters of Australia, where supplies and the assistance of shore-based aircraft would be available.

The campaign which followed would be one of commercial raiding accompanied by other forms of economic pressure against a Japan which would find herself debarred from access to supplies of oil, tin, rubber and iron without which she could not expect to conduct a lengthy war, since her considerable stockpiles of essential strategic raw materials must in due course be depleted. Japanese leaders would then be compelled to choose between eventual defeat by economic pressure or large-scale offensive naval operations designed to give them access to the oil and iron and other essential supplies located in the East Indies. Since they would be forced to take the initiative, the Japanese, it was argued, would be compelled to fight the decisive battles of such a campaign under conditions which would be decidedly unfavorable to them. The Japanese would be operating at considerable distance from home bases and their naval strength would be inferior to that which the United States could bring to bear against them, even if Great Britain were prevented by the situation in the Mediterranean or the Atlantic from appreciably reinforcing the reduced naval forces which the Royal Navy and the Royal Australian Navy had been maintaining in the south Pacific and Indian Oceans since the outbreak of war in Europe.

Advocates of some such scheme of United States naval strategy in the southwest Pacific, which implied a prior and a continuing agreement with Great Britain, Australia and New Zealand—

the details of the strategy doubtless varied from individual to individual—asserted their confidence that a clear indication of American intentions would probably suffice to prevent further Japanese pressure southward and might thus avoid war between Japan and the United States, while the latter might still pursue its dual policy of material aid to Great Britain in Europe and of financial assistance to China in Asia. If, however, the Japanese Government—under military or naval pressure—should prefer even a highly dangerous war in the southwest Pacific as the only face-saving alternative to the gradual frustration of its ambitions, the risks assumed by the United States would not be great despite the lack of specifically American bases in the southwest Pacific and the admittedly considerable distance of the strategic islands in that region from continental United States.

In appraising these risks, some attention also came to be given during the closing months of 1940 to the immediate and to the ultimate significance of the contribution which might be made to joint operations in the southwest Pacific by the Commonwealth of Australia and, to a lesser extent by its sister Dominion, New Zealand, as well as by the naval, air and land forces in the Netherlands Indies. The progress of Australian rearmament in the pre-war years, and, in its accelerated and considerably modified form during the first year of the war in Europe, came to receive some attention in unofficial as well as in official American circles; with that attention came an appreciation of both the active and the potential strategic contribution of Australia and New Zealand.

It has been remarked in the opening paragraph of this section that advocates of a special regional emphasis in pre-war Australian defense programs had been frowned upon by some of their fellow countrymen. The traditional twentieth century defense policy of Australia had been to emphasize the importance of the Royal Australian Navy upon which the greater part of the annual defense appropriations was expended. It was recognized that the Australian nation could not hope to provide itself with a navy capable of defending the island continent from successful attack by a first-class naval power which was free to concentrate the greater part of its forces in Australian waters. Heavy naval expenditure was, however, justified on the plea that Australia's contribution to British naval strategy might be decisive and might provide a nucleus for defensive action in the south Pacific or in the Indian Ocean, pending the arrival of British assistance. While this view dominated Australian defense programs before and in the two decades following the Great War, some provision had also been made for military defense forces. Compulsory training for home defense had been instituted in 1909 and maintained with some variations until 1929, when it was suspended by a Labor Government which disliked the idea of compulsion and which was also faced by the financial exigencies of the economic depression. As the events of the 'thirties increased the danger of war and also revealed the limitations of British naval strength in the Pacific, a school of Australian opinion emerged which stressed the need for greater emphasis upon the land and air defenses of Australia, including the local manufacture of munitions of war and of fighting planes and bombers. Political considerations retarded the application of this program which was felt by some to imply not only a weakening of the vitally important strategic association with the British Navy but also an assertion of an independent and isolationist foreign policy. There was nevertheless a steady increase in the pre-war Australian defense expenditure which rose from £A3,500,000 in 1933 to £A43,000,000 for a three-year defense program announced in March 1938. The importance of local production of munitions and airplanes was also emphasized by the establishment of a Ministry of Supply in April 1939. In the same month plans were made for the co-ordination of British, Australian and New Zealand defense in the Pacific at a conference which met at Wellington, New Zealand.

The outbreak of war and its course in 1940 led to a progressive increase in the tempo of Australian rearmament and brought about an appreciable change in the degree of emphasis placed on home defense and local manufacture of munitions. In 1914–18, the Australian contribution to the Allied war effort had consisted chiefly of man power—329,000 volunteers of the Australian Imperial Forces served abroad—and of raw materials. In the war which began in September 1939, Australian military and naval forces were destined once more to play a part overseas. Three divisions of an Expeditionary Force had been raised before the war was a year old and a fourth was on the point of formation. In September 1940, Australian soldiers were to be found in England, on the Mediterranean fronts and at Singapore. But it was clear that the situation of 1939–40 was very different from that of 1914–15. The situation on the home front was greatly changed. The danger was greater since Japan was a potential opponent instead of an ally, as previously; the material resources available for the war effort had also been vastly augmented by the rapid progress of Australian industrialization in the quarter of a century following the outbreak of the Great War of 1914. Under the spur of necessity following the *Blitzkrieg* in Europe, the conflict between regional and overseas defense conceptions was resolved.

A year after the outbreak of hostilities it was possible to state that, in addition to her overseas expeditionary divisions and to the activity of her naval units working in conjunction with the British Navy, Australia was maintaining her scheduled quota contributions under the Empire Air Scheme, in accordance with which she would send overseas 28,500 fully trained air crews and ground personnel by June 1941, the number rising to more than 57,000 by March 1943. This, independently of training and equipping the Royal Australian Air Force for service at home and in neighboring regions. By July 1940, the number of men trained or in training for the R.A.A.F., and for overseas air service, totalled 30,000. Lockheed-Hudson bombers had been ordered from the United States and a first instalment of 86 obtained by April 1940. Gipsy and Tiger Moth training planes were being manufactured in Australia, together with Wirraways, a plane designed to serve both for training purposes and for effective resistance against sea-borne aircraft. A start was also made with the local manufacture of heavy Beaufort bombers, the rate of production of which was being accelerated so that an output of one per week was officially predicted for 1941. A trained land force of 250,000 by the same year was planned with some 40,000 expeditionary force troops always in training in Australia as the nucleus of a home defense force which included compulsorily trained men of the ages 20–23, a voluntary militia and various forms of militia reserves consisting mainly of veterans of the Great War. For these air and land forces Australian factories were turning out rifles, machine guns, small tanks, shells and bombs; supplies were also being provided for New Zealand which lacks some of the mineral resources and the heavy industrial equipment available in Australia. For the Royal Australian Navy, additional destroyers were being built in Australian shipyards. Dock facilities were being improved and extended. Considerable sums were being spent on the naval base at Darwin in northern Australia and construction of a drydock for battleships was begun in Sydney Harbor with its completion planned for 1941–42.

New Zealand's wartime effort was no less significant in proportion to its total population of 1,624,000. In 1914–18, no less than 110,000 New Zealanders served overseas; in addition to the expeditionary forces organized shortly after the outbreak of war in September 1939, New Zealand also undertook its quota under the Empire Air Scheme, which was designed to insure that, when the scheme was fully operating, 3,700 trained air personnel would proceed overseas from New Zealand annually. That the naval contribution of New Zealanders was not negligible was demonstrated by the part of the cruiser *Achilles* in the Battle of the Plate which led to the destruction of the *Graf von Spee*. New Zealand's industrial development did not permit a munitions output similar to that of Australia, but engineering works were adapted to the production of light arms. The principle of conscription was accepted both for home and for overseas service.

The immediate bearing of Australian and New Zealand pre-war and wartime rearmament programs upon the strategic situation in the southwest Pacific was perhaps less than its long-term significance. If lasting Australian-American political and strategic collaboration in a joint policy for the Pacific were to emerge out of the peculiar pressures of the 1940 wartime situation, it was evident that a country which possessed adequate supplies of iron, coal, tin and copper; which retained free access to oil and rubber in the adjacent Indies; and which had steadily increased its overhead equipment for the manufacture of all classes of munitions, could do much to contribute to the permanent pacification of the Ocean at the southwest edge of which it stood as the central land mass—3,000 miles from east to west and 2,000 miles from north to south—among a scattered and wealthy group of islands. The direction of the whole of this region lay in the hands of people whose political ideas corresponded closely with those of the democracy which dominates the Ocean on its northeastern American shores. An aggressive nation which sought the hegemony of the Pacific could not fail to be influenced by the future strength of the southwestern group, notwithstanding the fact that the white population of Australia might not have moved much beyond its seven millions and that the distance from the southwestern to the northeastern shores of the Pacific was indeed considerable.

Even on a short view, it was possible for some American observers in September-December 1940 to emphasize the value of the contribution which could be made by Australia and New Zealand and especially by an Australian democracy which was geared to a considerable war effort, which had in fact become an important arsenal of the southwest Pacific and which could bring to joint defensive activity in that region military forces to aid in stiffening resistance of other troops, a not negligible and an increasing air force, constant supplies of raw materials and some finished war munitions acceptable even to allied forces, as well as some naval strength released from service elsewhere. In addition, the naval and seaplane bases of eastern and northern Australia might make a decisive difference to the transport of supplies and to the movement of American warships across the south Pacific out of the range of effective Japanese interference.

41

For these reasons, while the Australian people watched with great interest and considerable encouragement the swing of American opinion toward the southwest Pacific in the closing months of 1940, they did so without any sense of national inferiority due to the inevitable limitations which geographical situation and a limited manpower set to their actual or potential wartime effort. The gradual awakening of the nation to its external dangers had produced a new realist approach to Australian defense policy. Blind faith and confidence, on the one hand, and apathy and indifference, on the other, had given place to a realization of liabilities as well as of assets. Readiness to collaborate to the maximum with British operations in Europe had not prevented a healthy, if delayed orientation of Australian thought toward the Pacific, where lay the immediate threat to Australian security. As a result, the quickened interest of Australians in American policy in the Pacific was accompanied by a readiness for the greatest possible degree of political and strategic cooperation with the United States—with a nation whose resources were admittedly far greater than those of Australia and whose active friendship was, therefore, not only to be welcomed but even to be sought. But in seeking to transform an existing friendly relationship into one of active collaboration, possibly even to the point of joint defensive measures, Australians did not feel that they approached their American friends cap in hand, bearing nothing with them to place in a common pool. At the end of the first year of hostilities, the Australian was not in despair. He had recovered from the several shocks which had shaken him out of his provincial preoccupation with local problems. He had attained a high degree of national unity in support of an agreed defense program. By the end of 1940 he was conscious of considerable wartime achievement and, if anything, was over confident rather than defeatist in considering his future ability to contribute to his own defense.

This spirit in which the Australian at the end of 1940 approached not only his immediate war problems at home but also the future possibilities of collaboration with other peoples abroad, whom he respected and with whom he felt himself to have strategic interests as well as other things in common, may rightly be stressed in an appreciation of the strategic approach to Australian-American relations. For the Australian spirit was no negligible element in the contribution which Australia might bring to a common cause—as many American soldiers who were in France in 1918 were ready to testify. The Australian Minister to the United States voiced the feelings of the people as well as of the Government which he represented at Washington, when he declared on October 24, 1940, at the close of a widely reported and nationally broadcast address to the *New York Herald Tribune* Forum on "America's Second Fight for Freedom":

> If, at any time, Australia were called on to make its contribution to a general war effort in the southwestern Pacific, that contribution would be far from negligible. We have the natural resources; we have the industrial equipment to make effective use of those resources and we have the trained man power. Most important of all, however, is the spirit with which Australians would enter any struggle to defend their freedom and their independence from an aggressor who sought to dominate the southwestern Pacific. A few years ago, the Australian people, like the peoples of other democratic countries, were slow to realize the dangerous forces which were at work overseas. That, however, is of the past. Today, my countrymen are fully alive to the realities of the world situation; they know something of the sacrifices it may demand of them; I believe that they are ready to make those sacrifices, not blindly but with their eyes open. It is because my fellow countrymen are alive to the real nature of the moral issues at stake in the world today that they are determined to see through to the bitter end the struggle in which they are now engaged. We do not admit the possibility of defeat. For the struggle is to us, in very truth, a second fight for freedom.

V. ECONOMIC FACTORS

No apology is necessary for deferring a discussion of economic relations between the United States and Australia to a comparatively late stage in this analysis. Trade and commerce between the two countries has been considerable throughout the twentieth century, especially since the Great War of 1914-18. The trade has fluctuated violently, but American exports to Australia have increased to the point where, over the last decade, Australia has bought more from the United States than from any other single country except Great Britain. It is possible—indeed, it is highly probable—that the Australian market will become still more valuable to American exporters in the post-war period. The view has been expressed in Section IV above that the United States and Australia share a common economic and strategic interest in the raw materials of the East Indies. As will be suggested below, the two countries may also find a common interest in helping to create and to maintain the political conditions necessary for the development of other Pacific markets in which each may operate to advantage. It is nevertheless submitted that nothing is to be gained by pretending that Australia (or, for that matter, New Zealand) is likely to become a region of such vital material significance to the United States that, for economic reasons alone, its security and independence should ever be a major concern of the American people. The economies of the two countries are, in fact, competing rather than complementary. Consideration of the bearing of commercial conditions upon political relations should begin with a clear recognition of this fact.

The point having been made, it may readily be admitted (as

was implied in Section II above) that a very considerable contribution to the existing relationship between the United States and Australia has been made by American business enterprise. Apart from mere trading activities, credit must also be given to the stimulating influence of Americans in the development of Australian resources. It has been said that "the American invasion of Australia" dates from the Gold Rush days in Victoria in the 'fifties of the last century and still continues! In transport, in mining and in other engineering enterprises, Australia owes much to the initiative of individual Americans, some of whom have remained permanently in the country. When the European complications of 1914–18 lessened the flow of British and European goods to Australia, American as well as Japanese manufacturers profited by the absence of effective competition. After the war, many of them held their advantage. As the rising Australian tariffs of the post-war period challenged the foreign exporter in the interest of rapidly expanding Australian industries, some American concerns accepted the inevitable and withdrew from the Australian market; others established factories in Australia. On the eve of the second World War it was estimated that American investment in Australia (including Australian bonds held in New York) totalled at least half a billion dollars.

Meanwhile, despite tariff restrictions, American exports continued to reach high levels. These exports consisted of certain raw materials and of the output of some American heavy industries. Australia bought more American tobacco than any other country except Great Britain, the peacetime total running as high as $8,000,000 per year. Gasoline and oil imports exceeded $9,000,000 in annual value; automobiles—Australia makes her own car bodies but not, as yet, their engines—and industrial machinery accounted for $30,000,000; electrical machinery for some $3,000,000; chemicals a like amount, and agricultural machinery more than $6,000,000. In return, Australia succeeded in selling to the United States a certain amount of its fine wool, for mixture with coarser American-grown wool, hides and skins, lead and other minerals. That the "balance of trade" remained

45

heavily in favor of the United States is revealed by the following ten-year table:

AUSTRALIAN IMPORTS FROM AND EXPORTS TO THE UNITED STATES
(Excluding Gold Bullion Specie)

Years	Imports from U. S. A. to Australia (in £ sterling)	Exports from Australia to U. S. A. (in £ sterling)
1928–29	35,307,343	5,831,794
1929–30	30,313,535	4,233,772
1930–31	11,399,005	2,930,407
1931–32	7,037,417	1,990,262
1932–33	8,084,047	1,341,241
1933–34	7,838,982	2,491,601
1934–35	11,041,365	2,754,228
1935–36	13,901,705	5,615,372
1936–37	12,959,149	10,935,103
1937–38	17,758,684	3,383,508
1938–39	14,647,305	3,614,038

Australians have been concerned by their failure to increase substantially the proportion of sales to purchases. With, however, one striking exception in 1936–37 (when a short-lived attempt was made to divert trade from "bad customers" to "good customers") the adverse balance of trade produced no actual or potential political complications between the two countries. On the other hand, the determination of Australians to continue their industrial progress toward a more balanced economy made them reluctant to consider the possibility of increased sales of raw materials in the United States at the cost of serious limitations on Australian manufacturers.

The impact of the war upon the Australian economy in 1939 and 1940 did little to encourage hopes of great increases in the direct trade between the United States and Australia when the war was over. The immediate effect was to increase imports from the United States to aid Australian rearmament despite an acute shortage of dollar exchange and a consequential limitation of the import of luxuries and other "non-essential" American goods. Sales of Australian wool to the United States were retarded by the agreement by which the British Government bought the entire Australian wool clip for the duration of the war and one year thereafter. Though the agreement contained provisions for the resale by Great Britain of an unwanted surplus, some permanent loss in the American market was feared by Australian wool growers. It also seemed inevitable that the rapid acceleration of Australian heavy industries as part of the munitions program, referred to in the preceding section, must have the effect of limiting imports in the post-war period, as expanded wartime industries sought to adapt themselves to peacetime conditions by obtaining government protection from external competition.

In other respects, however, the economic effect of the war served to increase the interest of Australians in the future development of markets in the Pacific area. During the first few months of hostilities overseas, when the post-war thinking of Australians was based on the assumption of an Anglo-French victory leading to some form of closer union or association for the countries of Europe under British and French direction, there were not wanting those who predicted that the economic consequences of such European integration would necessarily tend to weaken the assured markets available to Australian raw materials in Great Britain. Since a balanced Australian economy was, at the best, a very distant possibility, expansion of Pacific markets, whether in China and in Japan or in southeastern Asia, would clearly be to the economic advantage of Australia. But such an expansion posited peace and security in the Pacific area. Economic considerations accordingly strengthened the trend of Australian thought which, for other reasons, was moving toward closer association with foreign countries bordering on the Pacific.

In specific relationship to the United States, Australians ventured to suggest that they might find a common economic bond with Americans in the advantage which exporting interests in both countries might secure from the increased consumption power of Asiatic peoples, if peace could be restored to the western Pacific and if the security of the Pacific could be underwritten by

47

some form of American and British (including Australian) collaboration.

In his inquiries throughout the year, the writer found little support in the United States for this argument. In the earlier part of the year the argument was frequently rejected with some vigor because it was associated with an earlier phase of American "imperialism" across the Pacific which had long been out of favor. Even business men who were approached failed to respond with any enthusiasm to talk regarding the future value of the Chinese market to American exporters. The prospect was too much of the future for those whose concern was with a return from their capital today or tomorrow, not many years ahead. In the new circumstances produced by the fall of France and the possibility of a Nazi-dominated Europe, a sensible modification of some American comment on trans-Pacific economic possibilities was discernible. Particularly in quarters where doubts were entertained regarding the feasibility of a Pan-American economic cartel, bargaining as a unit with a totalitarian Europe in regard to the surplus products of both the Americas, a revived interest in Asiatic markets could be detected. But it would be unwise to exaggerate the degree of this interest or the political pressure which it might be capable of exerting. The same should be said of the response to suggestions that post-war Australia might be increasingly attractive as a field of American capital investment and that American heavy industries might benefit considerably during the decades in which Australia was still further extending its secondary industrial activities. The writer found such suggestions accepted as possible lines of future economic association with Australia but, of themselves, as insufficient to carry the United States into political and strategic commitments in the southwest Pacific which might be a condition precedent to the maintenance of even pre-war American trade with Australia and New Zealand.

One argument designed to establish the existence of an important though indirect economic interest of the United States in the security and continued independence of Australia and New

48

Zealand deserves special consideration. If the economic counter-part of hemisphere defense implies the ability of the United States and the other countries of North and South America to act as a bargaining unit in regard to their export surpluses *vis-à-vis* those parts of the world under totalitarian control, it is argued that much will depend on the attitude toward the American bargaining unit of other countries with similar materials for export. If Australia and New Zealand were brought within the Japanese economic system as the result of Japanese control of the Netherlands Indies and Singapore—a control which would enable the Japanese Navy to block effective commercial com-munications between Australia and New Zealand and either America or Europe—this would mean that Australian and New Zealand wool, wheat, meat and dairy produce would be avail-able to a totalitarian Europe, by grace of Japan, at bedrock prices. The result would be a serious leak in any proposed western hemi-sphere economic system.

The reply that the addition of Australian and New Zealand surplus production to that of the Americas would create a unit too large to administer effectively may seem convincing, but it evokes the rejoinder that what the original argument sought to establish was that both the United States and the British Domin-ions in the southwest Pacific have a common interest in the development of new markets. The only way in which consider-able new markets may be located in the Pacific area is by restoring peace and providing security for the economic development of backward countries in the Pacific. For this, the argument con-cludes, some measure of British-American collaboration in the south west Pacific is essential. Indirectly, therefore, on economic as well as on cultural, political and strategic grounds, there is a case for closer relations between the United States and Australia.

VI. DOUBTS AND DIFFICULTIES

One advantage of the ease of intercourse and the friendly attitude which most Australians quickly enjoy in the United States, is that frank discussion of controversial issues involved in Australian-American relations is readily possible, even where it is clear that one party to the discussion has special interests at heart. For the greater part of a year the writer has been discussing with Americans, in one form or another, the substance of each of the preceding sections. It is fitting, therefore, to record some of the doubts and difficulties raised by Americans in those discussions, as well as to note other obstacles to closer relations with the United States which may be thought to lie in Australia itself.

One of the most serious and most common objections voiced by Americans took the form of an assertion that they would be truly shocked to see Australia's continued independence seriously threatened by a Japanese southward drive but that, for them, as Americans, the real danger is across the Atlantic, not across the Pacific. Since it is in the joint interest of the United States and of Great Britain—indeed, of all parts of the British Commonwealth—that the maximum American aid should be given to Great Britain in her resistance to Nazi aggression, no step should be taken by the United States in the western Pacific which might in any way limit the effectiveness of immediate or future aid to Britain. The argument has been expressed in different ways at different times. In the dark days of June, it frequently took the form of counselling open withdrawal from the Pacific and more or less active efforts to appease Japan, even, perhaps, by winking at a "temporary" domination of the East Indies. In more recent times, it has been consistent with a display of diplomatic hostility to Japan which could be made with the mental reservation that it should not carry the United States into any action likely to involve it in the risk of war in the Pacific.

It is difficult, emotionally as well as intellectually, for an Australian to take the allegedly long view of accepting Japanese domination of the whole of the western Pacific pending a Nazi defeat in Europe which might free Great Britain and the United States to undo the damage which had been done in the Pacific. Emotional complications apart, the argument does not seem to the writer to carry conviction for the very good reason that Japanese control of the whole of the western Pacific would weaken the prospect of British victory in Europe. There is fairly general agreement amongst Americans that British victory—which Gallup polls toward the end of 1940 revealed to be the expectation of the great majority of the American people—will come as the result of a deterioration in German morale and destruction of German resources by heavy bombing of German cities. This implies eventual British superiority in the air, to which American airplane factories will make a considerable contribution. An essential condition of that air superiority will, however, be trained airmen as well as airplanes. To this the Australian and New Zealand quotas under the Empire Air Scheme, mentioned in Section IV above, might well be decisive. Yet, unless the lanes of commerce are kept open in the Pacific as well as in the Atlantic, neither Australian airmen nor Australian raw materials could reach Great Britain. Given Japanese domination of the East Indies and Singapore, Australian and New Zealand communications overseas would be at the mercy of the Asiatic ally of the European totalitarian powers. To that extent British air superiority would be endangered. Provision of Australian, New Zealand and Indian reinforcements and supplies to the eastern Mediterranean would also be precluded. An American policy of inaction in the western Pacific would thus defeat its declared end. Appeasement, like peace, is indivisible.

A second objection, frequently expressed, is that though Americans might wish to stop further Japanese aggression in the southwest Pacific, the United States could, in fact, do nothing without great risk because of the great distances involved and because of the lack of adequate bases west of Hawaii. A war in Japanese home waters, against a fleet whose fighting strength is not fully known, at a time when the United States "two-ocean" navy is not yet in being, represents too great and too costly an effort to be contemplated while the outcome of the situation across the Atlantic remains uncertain. This objection has already been considered in Section IV above, where attention has been drawn to the emergence of a new emphasis on the significance of a more defensive policy, a "holding war" in the south west Pacific, which would not entail the same risks for the United States Navy. Adoption of such a policy, preceded by some United States-British (including Australian and New Zealand) understanding or agreement, and clearly known to the Japanese might, in fact, avoid war. If hostilities should result, the strain upon United States naval forces would not be so great as necessarily to preclude continuance of a measure of assistance to Great Britain in Europe.

A more serious, yet, in its way, a clarifying criticism of the thesis of the preceding pages is provided by some Americans who take their stand frankly on the ground that, while they would be genuinely distressed to see Australia fall under Japanese domination, American policy must be based on American interests—and the United States has no vital interests in the western Pacific. In the writer's view, this criticism suggests the right line of approach to the strategic issues involved in Australian-American relations. Closer political association or strategic collaboration cannot come unless Australians and Americans are convinced that they have vital interests in common. Effective cooperation will not come from sentiment alone. It is not surprising that Australians should today recognize certain interests in the Pacific as vital and that they should regard these interests as common both to themselves and to Americans. Living as they do in a troubled world in which their distance from Europe has become more of a liability than an asset, Australians have indeed been shocked out of their preoccupation with local affairs and

52

out of their excessive confidence in European succor in an hour of need. They cannot, however, neglect the fact that there are Americans—not so many, perhaps, as in 1939 and in the first half of 1940, but a sizable group—who believe that the United States could manage well enough if all Europe fell under Nazi control and all countries in the western and south western Pacific were subject to Japan. To such Americans, if they are sincerely and honestly prepared to face a lowering of the American standard of living and if they are ready to surrender any claim to an American role of international leadership, accepting in its stead a relationship with foreign countries which would depend on the grace of powerful dictators or on the opportunist exploitation of diplomatic advantage—to these there is nothing which an Australian should say. To those other Americans who are ready to shoulder responsibilities in defense of what they can clearly accept as American national interests in the Pacific, two things at least may be said even by a foreign observer.

The first is that the region of the southwest Pacific is one from which at present the United States draws strategic raw materials which are vital to the continuance of American rearmament and therefore to the continuance of the United States as a great world power. It may be granted that this dependence might be minimized by determined attention to the production of synthetic rubber regardless of cost, and to the discovery of substitutes for tin. Until this determination has clearly manifested itself, the southwest Pacific remains an area, assured access to which is a matter of vital importance to the United States. No American should lull himself into a sense of false security by accepting the argument, commonly voiced in the middle of 1940, that a Japanese-dominated East Indies and Malaya would still be ready and anxious to sell tin and rubber to the United States. Undoubtedly they would—until it suited the political or strategic interest to Japan to close the door abruptly.

The second thing which may be said of the strategic significance to the United States of the southwest Pacific is that Japanese control of the region would not only force the United

States to look elsewhere for vital war materials but would also free Japan from an acute dependence on external supplies of oil and iron, without both of which no Japanese Government could conduct a lengthy modern war. Control of the southwest Pacific would accordingly transform the trans-Pacific ally of the potential European rivals of the United States from an important manufacturing nation with considerable naval strength but with seriously limited natural resources, into a truly formidable and substantially self-sufficient Pacific power. That this direct material interest of the United States in the southwest Pacific may also be reinforced by an indirect economic concern for the fate of Australia and New Zealand has also been suggested in the preceding section.

At this point in the writer's discussions with American friends it has not been uncommon for one of them to turn the argument from American to Australian policy. "If you think there is a case for Australian-American cooperation and if you are disposed to stress the importance for the United States of maintaining the *status quo* in the Netherlands Indies and in neighboring regions, how can you reconcile this with the fact that your own country has continued to play ball with Japan? Was it not Australia which tried to perpetuate the Anglo-Japanese Alliance in 1921? Is there not evidence to suggest that Australia has encouraged recent British efforts to 'appease' Japan?"

To such questions an Australian might give two answers. Insofar as the issue concerns the short-term needs of his country he would insist that no Australian Government in recent years could afford to ignore either the limited naval assistance upon which it might with confidence rely, or the exposed position in which it would be placed, in the event of a war between Japan and the nations of the British Commonwealth. It may be repeated that Australians of necessity approach the subject of Japan's relations with foreign powers in terms of Australia's own immediate security. No other approach is possible for a white population of seven millions resident a month's sailing distance from Great Britain and nearly three weeks from America. Gestures of American sympathy, after attack by overwhelming Asiatic force, would be small consolation to Australians for temerity in having needlessly provoked a powerful neighbor. But change the premises and the conclusion would change with them. There are few Australians who would hesitate to predict with confidence that, if the people of the United States were prepared to support their Government in joint action against Japanese aggression in the southwest Pacific, the Australian Government would accompany the United States in every measure, diplomatic or otherwise, which was designed to maintain the *status quo* in the Pacific against violent disturbance by the armed force of Japan or of any other power.

The Australian's reply to criticism of his country's humoring of Japan should not, however, stop at this point. His second comment should be to remark upon the growth of a school of Australian opinion which interprets the situation in the Far East as the result not only of the ambition of the Japanese but also of the selfishness of others, including Australians and Americans, in denying to the Japanese effective opportunities in other markets. In other words, Australian policy in the Pacific, in its more enlightened moments, has been based on more than a desire not to provoke Japan to action which it would be beyond Australian capacity to resist unaided. It has also been groping its way toward a more comprehensive Pacific settlement which would provide a basis for permanent peace and prosperity in the Pacific. In so doing, Australians have been reluctant to accept the view that this basis can only be found at the expense of Japan and after an "inevitable war" with that country. On the contrary, they have looked hopefully to the revival and extension of a mutually advantageous economic relationship between Australia and Japan.

Some Australian, as well as some American readers may be disposed to decry the last few sentences as a rationalization after the event of what was largely an opportunist attempt of Australian governments to avoid serious danger in their increasingly exposed position in the late 'thirties. It is also possible that formal Japanese association with the Axis Powers has increased the risk of war. It is nevertheless worth insisting that, despite occasional reappearance of the Japanese bogy in Australia, there is much less anti-Japanese feeling in Australia than is to be found in all parts of the United States, north, south, east and west. If the Australian could be kept from relapsing into his provincial distaste for any foreign commitments he would be ready to enter somewhat dispassionately into any Pacific negotiations which involved not merely his own immediate security but also a settlement of conflicting ambitions of the non-white peoples of the Pacific. It is worth insisting that one of the basic difficulties in Australian-American relations may be found to lie in certain differences of emotional approach to the Far East.

From this follows the suggestion that there is more to the problem of political relations between the United States and Australia than the securing of some *modus vivendi* which each might accept under pressure of wartime necessity. On a long view, one of the greatest dangers is the possibility that when the present war is over both Australian and American nations may rapidly revert to type in their attitude to foreign affairs—as each of them did in 1919 and after. It is, of course, possible to argue that the lessons of 1940 have been so sharp that their mark will remain; that Americans will continue to think more of outer than of inner lines of defense, that Australians will retain their belated awareness of their Pacific environment. So may it be. But the prospect of continued closer association of the United States and Australia will depend not a little on the degree of long-range thinking which is allowed to enter into the discussion of immediate problems. These immediate problems must necessarily be the primary concern of the officials who are responsible for the conduct of a wartime government in the one country and of something closely resembling that in the other. Unofficial observers may, however, range more widely and should take every opportunity to press consideration of fundamental issues upon the respective governments in their relations with one another.

Among these fundamental questions the nature of the permanent organization of the Pacific area is one of great significance. Its importance is not likely to be ignored in a country like the United States where powerful pressure groups exist to serve certain viewpoints regarding the Far East and where other more detached bodies have already done much to bring Pacific problems before the United States Government and the American people. There is greater need and far less available machinery for the long-term task of preparing the Australian and the American peoples for that deeper understanding of one another which is an essential condition of permanently closer collaboration between them.

VII. CONDITIONS OF FUTURE COOPERATION

Since prediction of future trends in American or Australian opinion is confessedly excluded from the purpose of this essay, the section which follows is in some respects an anti-climax. For the reader whose interest is confined to the present and to the immediate future it would probably suffice to conclude with a warning against over-confident expectation that the rapid progress in Australian-American relations during the concluding months of 1940 will continue at the same rate and without interruption. Some such warning is, indeed, desirable in any case. A pendulum which swings sharply in one direction may swing back just as far. It should not invite the label of pessimist to suggest that certain changes in either the European or the Asiatic scene might have the effect of deflecting attention of Australians no less than of Americans from their relations with one another. A series of victories in the Mediterranean which freed a portion of the British Navy for service in the Pacific might not be without its influence on Australian opinion; conversely, persistent and heavy losses to British convoys in the Atlantic would inevitably revive American concern at possible action in the Pacific which might lessen ability to aid Great Britain in or across the Atlantic. The subject of Australian-American relations is, in short, of long-term as well as short-term significance. Even while the march of events is accomplishing more than could have been expected from the careful planning of men, that planning should continue. It may even be that the conditions of permanent progress in Australian-American relations will be found to lie elsewhere than in the exciting incidents of wartime defensive association.

Machinery to ensure a steady growth of contacts and understanding between the two countries should, of course, begin with political organization and may be greatly strengthened by semi-governmental activities. But it should not stop there. The beneficial results which have followed the diplomatic representation of Australia in Washington and of the United States in Canberra have already been indicated in the preceding pages. These results could doubtless be broadened and deepened by activities designed to increase the information available not only to the Government of the United States but also to special groups of American citizens interested in particular fields of Australian life, economic and otherwise, as well as to the public at large. Reference has been made to recent improvements in Australian press representation in America. It may be expected that this will continue and that Australian news will also receive greater prominence in American papers as the governmental relations between the United States and Australia are further strengthened. The writer nevertheless attaches considerable importance to steps which might be taken by private citizens and unofficial organizations in both countries. These might do much to improve the mutual knowledge and the understanding of the American and the Australian peoples, which is a condition precedent to permanent collaboration between them. Such activities do not require official endorsement or direction, though they would not suffer from a governmental blessing.

The need for improvement in knowledge and understanding of American thought and of American institutions in Australia has already been remarked. The cultural indifference of many Australians toward the United States has in the past been a serious obstacle to any organic relationship between the two countries. This indifference may in the long run be countered most effectively in the schools and universities of the several Australian States. Australian curricula at the tertiary no less than in the primary and secondary stages are heavily weighted toward Australian and European rather than Pacific and American affairs. This criticism may be made the more sharply since it is in part self-criticism. It happens to be part of the writer's professional responsibility to influence, though not necessarily to determine, the historical studies of future citizens of Western Australia, both in secondary schools and at the University. His experience of the last twelve months has made him uncomfortably conscious of the limited emphasis which he has given to studies which are essential to provide an informed background for intelligent adult appreciation of issues in Australian-American relations. It is no consolation to reflect that, in this, he has sinned in highly respectable company. It would in fact be difficult to find an Australian university which provides adequate facilities for the study of American history or of American civilization—and this despite a healthy orientation of some Australian university curricula toward the Pacific in recent years. Here is one field in which Australians owe it to themselves to see that the foundations of a better understanding are laid without delay. A stimulus in the right direction would be provided by the endowment, whether by Australian or by American funds, from official or exclusively unofficial sources, of a Chair of American History—or, better still, of American Civilization—in one of the six State universities or at the Canberra University College which is designed to become, among other things, a national research center.

It is not enough, however, that Australian children should receive elementary instruction in American affairs or that more advanced courses should be available to students in American universities. The time is long overdue for improved facilities for Australian post-graduate students to work for higher degrees in American as well as in British and European universities, as hitherto they have done almost exclusively, especially in political, social and cultural subjects. It is probably true to say that a readiness to encourage this will now be found among most of the professors and executive heads of the Australian universities; the main obstacles are financial and administrative. The problems presented by the greater cost of transport to the United States than to Great Britain (where ocean tourist travel facilities are available) and by higher living costs in the United States are not negligible but they should not be insuperable. It is desirable also that American students should work in Australia. While Australian universities could not expect to attract large numbers of American post-graduate students, the Australian scene provides special advantages for Americans interested in certain economic, social, anthropological and geological questions. An interesting proposal affecting younger students and suitable even for wartime adoption was made to the writer by a Swarthmore professor. It was suggested that an arrangement might well be made for American students to take one year of their four years of undergraduate study in Australian or New Zealand universities as part of a special course devised in American colleges to include study of Pacific problems.

Closely related with visits by Australian and American students is the proposal for exchange of university professors and of teachers in secondary and in elementary schools. There are obvious limits to the number of such exchanges but there would seem to be no reason why organized efforts by some constituted educational authority on either side of the Pacific should not produce greater results than are at present possible by the haphazard methods of a few individuals aided by the generosity of certain Foundations. The exchange of professors and teachers might also be extended to ministers of religion. There are already some Australian-born ministers in charge of churches in the United States and there have been some famous instances of American ministers who have served for a period in Australia. No difficulty other than financial would appear to prevent an extension of this practice, with results which should be highly advantageous to the peoples of both countries. Reference has already been made to the powerful influence which missionary activity in China and Japan has had upon American public opinion in regard to the western and north western Pacific. It is perhaps regrettable that the writer's regard for the truth prevents him from recommending an America-wide campaign to depict the spread of heathenish practices among the Australian people. There is something to be said for the view that, if the attention of American missionary societies could in this way be drawn to Australia, the problem of Australian-American relations would be solved for all time!

One barrier to better knowledge of Australian affairs in the United States, to which Americans have frequently drawn the writer's attention, is the difficulty of securing easy access to books and documents covering all sides of Australian life. This is a matter in which the aid of trained librarians might be sought. Better co-ordination in supplying current material from Australian government and semi-official departments appears to be indicated. Something might also be done to assist the marketing in the United States of the best books published in Australia. There seems no reason why some of the best Australian fiction of recent years should not be acceptable to American readers. An arrangement has been suggested between some of the larger Australian publishers and an American firm which might receive sheets of books deemed suitable for publication in American editions. Since it is difficult for Australian writers of short stories to find an opening in the overstocked and perhaps monopolistic American magazine market, the best way of getting Australian scenes familiar to the large magazine reading public in the United States would probably be by inducing more American writers to visit Australia and write against an Australian background. Much more might also be done through the use of the sound film.

The tourist traffic to and from Australia is an important aid to closer relations, but its significance should not be overrated. It affects a comparatively small section of either population and is confined almost exclusively to higher income range groups. The American tourist business is directed specifically at middle-aged and elderly persons and is based on the assumption that Americans cannot afford the time for a three months' vacation, necessary to make the trip to Australia and New Zealand, until they are at least middle-aged. The excellent American steamship service between California, Auckland, Sydney and Melbourne is accordingly designed for first-class passengers who can pay relatively high rates. One indirect result of the fact that there are no tourist-class steamers on this run is that Australians of middle income groups (and lower), who occasionally visit England, Scotland, Wales or Ireland, are discouraged from going or returning *via* America by the difference between the trans-Pacific and trans-America fares and the comparatively cheap rates available on English mailboats proceeding *via* Suez or round the Cape of Good Hope.

It is, of course, possible to argue that Australians should be encouraged to visit the United States as an alternative to "a trip Home", as even the most patriotic Australian is apt to describe a visit to Great Britain. To some, indeed, such an alternative is readily acceptable. In the main, however, Australian travelers are likely to continue to be drawn to Europe even after the present war. It is worth suggesting, moreover, that there is no special merit in seeking to build up Australian-American relations by trying to break through British-Australian or, for that matter, European-American associations. Educational and other activities designed to make Australians and Americans better known to one another should not aim at making the two identical.

The point is worth stressing for there is a group of Americans whose anxiety to see the United States more closely associated with the British Dominions in the southwest Pacific appears to be equalled only by their desire to reduce to a minimum their own associations with Great Britain and with Europe. The implication of their attitude is that all would be well for Australians and New Zealanders if only they would cut the painter, set themselves up as independent democracies—and, it seems, hope for the best. It is submitted that this view of Australian-American relations ignores a factor of race and sentiment which in the past has influenced and which, reinforced by other factors, will continue to influence the Australian attitude to the British Commonwealth. To ignore the mental attitude and the traditions which link Australians with Great Britain is as dangerous to clear thinking on the question of Australian-American relations as it would be to thrust aside the influences which make the United States of today so different in its attitude to Europe from the Atlantic coast colonies of the first half of the eighteenth century. The United States and Australia have many things in common; they are nevertheless distinct and different communities, each with its own past and, it may be assumed, with its own future. The writer sees no inconsistency between a belief that closer relations between the United States and Australia are possible and desirable, in the mutual interest of both countries, and a conviction that the continued existence of the British Commonwealth of Nations is of vital importance to Australia. He would like to believe that most Americans accept its continuance as significant for them also. At least he would suggest that to make Australian-American relations conditional on the collapse of the British Commonwealth is a false—he would venture to add—a fatal approach to the subject of this essay.

The argument may be carried one stage further. It is the writer's belief that the relations between the United States and Australia are not exclusively regional in character. Both countries have special interests in the Pacific region; each might contribute much to the future regional organization of the Pacific. It is nevertheless worth remembering that each country has in the past looked more to Europe than to Asia. It was the war in Europe rather than the war in Asia which brought the governments of the two countries more closely together in the second half of 1940 than they had ever been before. It is not reasonable to suggest that Europe will cease to loom large to both nations when the present wars are over. None can foretell how post-war Europe will fit into the world picture. It may be that the leadership in international relations will have passed from the old world to the new. If so, the success of Australian-American cooperation will be in a very real sense a measure of the sense of international responsibility which is to be found both in Australia and in the United States.

A purely *ad hoc* defensive arrangement in the southwest Pacific, such as seemed possible at any moment when these pages went to press, would not, of itself, be enough. It might be warmly welcomed for the increased sense of security it would provide in an hour of crisis but its long-term significance would depend on whether it was to prove the basis on which might be built a permanent regional association in the Pacific area as a whole. The prospect of success of such an association would be slight if the Australian and the American peoples of the new postwar period turned their backs on the rest of the world and reverted to something like their state of mind in 1920 and in the years that followed the end of the first World War.

It is because there is some evidence to suggest that the present wars in Europe and in Asia have produced among Australians and Americans a certain quickening sense of international responsibilities, as well as—in part, because of—a clearer view of material interests, that this analysis of Australian-American relations may conclude on a note of restrained optimism. The closer association of the United States and Australia, which has been a striking feature of the second half of 1940, may thus be welcomed in the name of international morality as well as in the interest of national security.

BIBLIOGRAPHY

A SHORT LIST OF BOOKS ON AUSTRALIAN AFFAIRS

GENERAL:

The Australian Encyclopaedia. 2 vols. 1925–26. Sydney, Angus & Robertson.

The Cambridge History of the British Empire. Vol. VII, Part I. "Australia." 1933. Cambridge University Press. Invaluable for the student though necessarily uneven in quality and not up-to-date.

Green, H. M. *An Outline of Australian Literature*. 1930. Sydney, Whitcombe & Tombs, Ltd.

Hancock, W. K. *Australia*. 1931. New York, C. Scribner's Sons. Still the best introductory analysis of Australian life and thought.

McGuire, Paul. *Australia, Her Heritage, Her Future*. 1939. New York, Frederick A. Stokes.

The Official Year Book of the Commonwealth of Australia. Canberra. An informative and attractive annual source book with more than statistical data.

POLITICAL:

Campbell, P., Mills, R. C. and Portus, G. V., Editors. *Studies in Australian Affairs*. 1928. Melbourne, Macmillan & Co., Ltd., in association with the Melbourne University Press.

Duncan, W. G. K., Editor. *Australia's Foreign Policy*. 1938. Sydney, Angus & Robertson. The proceedings of a conference of the Australian Institute of Political Science.

Harris, H. L. *Australia's National Interests and National Policy*. 1938. Melbourne, Melbourne University Press in association with Oxford University Press. Written in preparation for the unofficial conference of Institutes of International Affairs, held at Lapstone, N. S. W. in September 1938.

Shepherd, J. *Australia's Interests and Policies in the Far East*. 1940. New York, Institute of Pacific Relations, Inquiry Series.

ECONOMIC AND SOCIAL:

The Annals of the American Association of Political and Social Science, Philadelphia. November 1931. "An Economic Survey of Australia."

Eggleston, F. W., and others. *Australian Standards of Living*. 1939. Melbourne, Melbourne University Press in association with Oxford University Press. Sponsored by the Institute of Pacific Relations.

Phillips, P. D., and others. *The Peopling of Australia*. 1933. Melbourne, Melbourne University Press in association with Oxford University Press. A useful collection of essays.

Portus, G. V. *An Economic Interpretation of Australia*. 2nd Edition. 1933. Sydney, Angus & Robertson. A short, simply phrased but penetrating analysis.

Shann, E. O. G. *An Economic History of Australia*. 1930. Cambridge University Press. The standard and the only comprehensive work of its kind.

Wadham, S. M. and Wood, G. L. *Land Utilisation in Australia*. 1939. Melbourne, Melbourne University Press in association with Oxford University Press. Sponsored by the Institute of Pacific Relations.

PERIODICALS:

The Austral-Asiatic Bulletin. Melbourne, Victoria Branch of Australian Institute of International Affairs. Every second month. The best political journal published in Australia.

The Australian Quarterly. Sydney. The journal of the Australian Institute of Political Science.

The Economic Record. Melbourne University Press. The semi-annual journal of the Economic Society of Australia and New Zealand. A specialist publication of high quality.

The Round Table. London. The Australian articles in this British Commonwealth quarterly provide the most connected chronicle of Australian events. Though dispassionately presented, they are sometimes colored by a conservative viewpoint in local politics. There is no Labor periodical of high standard to which reference can be made for the opposing viewpoint.

N.B. A comprehensive bibliography will be found in the volume of the *Cambridge History of the British Empire* cited above.